Yungblud

Chapter 1: Introduction

Yungblud, a name that has become synonymous with rebellion, authenticity, and boundary-pushing in the music industry, rose to fame as a voice for the disenfranchised youth of today. But behind the stage name lies Dominic Richard Harrison, a young man hailing from the vibrant town of Doncaster, South Yorkshire.

Born on August 5, 1997, Dominic, from an early age, displayed a vibrant energy and creative spirit that would later define his persona as Yungblud. However, his journey to stardom was not without its challenges.

Growing up in Doncaster, Dominic faced the typical trials and tribulations of adolescence. Yet, amidst the ordinary struggles, there was an extraordinary spark of talent waiting to be ignited. Little did he know that his unconventional path would lead him to become one of the most influential voices in contemporary music.

In this book, we will delve into the remarkable journey of Yungblud, from his humble beginnings in Doncaster to his meteoric rise to fame on the global stage. We will explore the influences, experiences, and pivotal moments that shaped Dominic Harrison into the rebel icon known as Yungblud, capturing the essence of his music, activism, and enduring impact on popular culture.

As Dominic navigated through his formative years in Doncaster, his vibrant personality often clashed with the conventional expectations of society. Diagnosed with attention deficit hyperactivity disorder (ADHD) at a young age, Dominic found himself labeled as a troublesome student, misunderstood due to his energetic nature and outspoken opinions.

Despite the challenges he faced, Dominic's passion for expression and creativity remained undeterred. His love for music became a beacon of solace and inspiration, providing an outlet for his thoughts, emotions, and rebellious spirit. It was during these formative years that the seeds of Yungblud were sown, laying the foundation for an extraordinary journey ahead.

In the following chapters, we will delve deeper into Dominic's evolution from a spirited youth in Doncaster to the charismatic force known as Yungblud. We will unravel the threads of his musical influences, explore the pivotal moments that shaped his career, and uncover the driving forces behind his unwavering commitment to authenticity, activism, and social change.

Join us on a journey through the life and legacy of Yungblud, where the lines between artistry and activism blur, and where rebellion becomes a rallying cry for a generation in search of truth, acceptance, and belonging.

Dominic's transition from a spirited youth in Doncaster to the enigmatic persona of Yungblud was not a straightforward one. Along the way, he encountered setbacks, doubts, and moments of self-discovery that would shape his identity as an artist and activist.

Through his music, Dominic found a voice to articulate the struggles, frustrations, and aspirations of his generation. He channeled his raw emotions and unfiltered thoughts into lyrics that resonated with audiences worldwide, sparking a movement that transcended genres and defied societal norms.

As we embark on this exploration of Yungblud's journey, we invite you to delve into the depths of his artistry, to uncover the layers of complexity that define his music, and to witness the transformation of a young dreamer from Doncaster into a global icon for change.

Join us as we unravel the enigma of Yungblud, from the streets of South Yorkshire to the stages of the world's biggest music festivals, where his message of rebellion, resilience, and revolution continues to reverberate with the hearts and minds of a generation yearning for something more.

Chapter 2: Early Life and Education

From an early age, Dominic Richard Harrison, known to the world as Yungblud, displayed a vibrant energy and creative spirit that set him apart from his peers. However, his journey through childhood was marked by challenges that would ultimately shape his path as an artist and activist.

Dominic's struggles with attention deficit hyperactivity disorder (ADHD) were evident from a young age. While his boundless energy and passion for expression were assets in many ways, they also made him a misunderstood figure in the traditional school environment. Despite his best efforts, Dominic often found himself at odds with the rigid structure of academia, where his lively demeanor was perceived as disruptive rather than inventive.

One pivotal moment came with Dominic's suspension from Ackworth School, a consequence of a dare from a friend that led to an act of defiance against authority. This incident highlighted the disconnect between Dominic's free-spirited nature and the expectations of the educational system, setting the stage for a journey of self-discovery and rebellion.

Determined to pursue his passion for the arts, Dominic embarked on a new chapter in his education at the Arts Educational Schools in London. Here, amidst the bustling creativity of the city, Dominic found a sanctuary where his unconventional talents were celebrated rather than stifled. It was within the walls of this institution that Dominic honed his skills as a performer, laying the groundwork for his future endeavors in music and acting.

In the next chapter of his life, Dominic would channel his experiences and struggles into a form of expression that transcended boundaries and resonated with audiences around the world. Through his music, he would defy expectations, challenge stereotypes, and inspire a generation to embrace their uniqueness and authenticity. But before the stage lights and adoring fans, there was a spirited young boy from Doncaster, navigating the complexities of adolescence with courage and determination.

Despite the challenges he faced, Dominic's journey through childhood and education was not solely defined by struggle. Within the chaos of his energetic nature and the frustrations of navigating a system ill-equipped to accommodate his unique talents, there existed moments of clarity and revelation.

It was during these formative years that Dominic began to recognize the power of his creativity as both a source of rebellion and a path to self-discovery. Through music, art, and performance, he found avenues of expression that transcended the limitations of traditional education, offering glimpses of a world where his boundless energy was not a liability, but a gift.

The suspension from Ackworth School, while initially perceived as a setback, became a catalyst for Dominic's transformation. Freed from the constraints of conformity, he embraced his identity as a nonconformist and embarked on a journey of exploration and growth.

At the Arts Educational Schools in London, Dominic found himself immersed in a vibrant community of artists, musicians, and performers who embraced diversity and celebrated individuality. Here, he discovered a sense of belonging that had eluded him in more traditional educational settings, surrounded by kindred spirits who understood and appreciated his unbridled creativity.

It was within the nurturing environment of Arts Ed that Dominic's talents began to flourish, laying the groundwork for his future endeavors in music and acting. As he honed his skills and explored new forms of expression, Dominic began to envision a future where his passion for art and activism could converge, creating a platform for social change and cultural revolution.

In the chapters to come, we will delve deeper into Dominic's journey as Yungblud, tracing the evolution of his music, activism, and impact on popular culture. But first, we must understand the formative experiences and influences that shaped the young rebel from Doncaster into the icon known as Yungblud.

Chapter 3: Career Beginnings

With a foundation laid in the vibrant arts community of London, Dominic Richard Harrison embarked on a journey of artistic exploration that would ultimately lead him to the forefront of the music industry as Yungblud. But before the stage lights and sold-out concerts, Dominic first found himself drawn to the world of acting.

Driven by a desire to express himself through various forms of art, Dominic initially pursued opportunities in acting, landing roles in television series such as Emmerdale and The Lodge. These early experiences provided Dominic with a taste of the entertainment industry and ignited a passion for performance that would shape his artistic journey.

However, it was music that truly captured Dominic's heart and soul, offering a platform for self-expression and connection that resonated with his rebellious spirit. Inspired by a diverse range of musical influences, Dominic began to experiment with songwriting and performance, blending elements of alternative rock, hip hop, and pop punk to create a sound that was uniquely his own.

In April 2017, Dominic took a bold step forward with the release of his debut single, "King Charles." The song, with its infectious energy and raw emotion, showcased Dominic's talent as a songwriter and performer, earning him critical acclaim and a dedicated following of fans.

Building on the success of "King Charles," Dominic continued to push boundaries and defy expectations with subsequent releases. In September 2017, he unveiled "I Love You, Will You Marry Me," a poignant ode to modern love that captured the hearts of listeners around the world.

But it was the release of "Tin Pan Boy" in November 2017 that truly marked a breakthrough moment for Dominic. The song, inspired by the construction project on Tin Pan Alley in London, showcased Dominic's ability to tackle social issues with wit and insight, cementing his reputation as a fearless voice for change.

As Dominic's music began to resonate with audiences on a global scale, he realized that he had found his true calling as Yungblud. With each new release, he continued to push the boundaries of creativity and authenticity, carving out a unique space for himself in the music industry and inspiring a new generation of artists and activists to follow in his footsteps.

Buoyed by the positive reception to his early singles, Dominic Richard Harrison, now fully immersed in his musical persona as Yungblud, embraced his newfound role as a boundary-pushing artist. With a penchant for blending genres and an unapologetic approach to tackling social issues, Yungblud quickly gained momentum in the music scene.

Following the success of "King Charles," "I Love You, Will You Marry Me," and "Tin Pan Boy," Yungblud's trajectory in the music industry continued to ascend. His electrifying live performances and dynamic stage presence earned him a reputation as a captivating performer, drawing audiences in with his infectious energy and raw emotion.

As Yungblud's fan base grew, so too did his ambition. In January 2018, he took another significant step in his career with the release of his debut EP, simply titled "Yungblud." The EP, featuring his early singles along with new tracks, served as a manifesto of sorts, introducing listeners to Yungblud's fearless approach to music and storytelling.

With tracks like "Polygraph Eyes," a powerful commentary on sexual assault, and "Loner," an anthem for outsiders and misfits, Yungblud established himself as a voice for the voiceless, unafraid to tackle taboo subjects and challenge societal norms.

But it was his debut studio album, "21st Century Liability," released in July 2018, that truly solidified Yungblud's place in the music industry. The album, a bold and unapologetic exploration of the struggles facing young people in the modern world, struck a chord with audiences worldwide, earning widespread critical acclaim and spawning hits like "Falling Skies" and "Psychotic Kids."

As Yungblud's star continued to rise, he embarked on a relentless touring schedule, captivating audiences with his electrifying live performances and unwavering commitment to authenticity. With each new release, he pushed the boundaries of his artistry, refusing to be confined by genre or convention.

In the next chapter, we will explore Yungblud's continued evolution as an artist, from his collaborations with other musicians to his growing impact on popular culture and activism. Join us as we delve deeper into the world of Yungblud, where music becomes a catalyst for change and rebellion is a way of life.

Chapter 4: 21st Century Liability Era

With the release of his debut studio album, "21st Century Liability," Yungblud cemented his position as one of the most fearless and innovative voices in contemporary music. Released in July 2018, the album served as a powerful commentary on the struggles facing young people in the modern world, tackling issues such as mental health, societal pressures, and the pervasive influence of social media.

"21st Century Liability" was more than just an album; it was a manifesto for a generation grappling with the complexities of the digital age. Through his music, Yungblud gave voice to the frustrations, fears, and hopes of young people everywhere, offering a cathartic outlet for self-expression and solidarity.

The album was met with widespread critical acclaim, earning praise for its bold lyricism, infectious energy, and genre-defying sound. Tracks like "Polygraph Eyes," a haunting reflection on sexual assault and consent, and "Loner," an anthem for outsiders and misfits, struck a chord with audiences around the world, resonating with their raw honesty and emotional depth.

But the success of "21st Century Liability" was not without its challenges. As Yungblud continued to push the boundaries of his artistry, he faced criticism and backlash from some quarters, with detractors dismissing his music as too provocative or controversial. Yet, for Yungblud, controversy was never a deterrent; it was a badge of honor, a sign that he was making an impact and challenging the status quo.

Despite the challenges, "21st Century Liability" became a rallying cry for a generation in search of truth, authenticity, and belonging. Its impact reverberated far beyond the confines of the music industry, inspiring a new wave of activism and social change.

In the next chapter, we will explore Yungblud's journey beyond "21st Century Liability," from his collaborations with other musicians to his growing influence on popular culture and activism. Join us as we delve deeper into the world of Yungblud, where music becomes a catalyst for change and rebellion is a way of life.

Despite any challenges it faced, "21st Century Liability" continued to resonate deeply with audiences, solidifying Yungblud's reputation as a boundary-pushing artist unafraid to confront societal issues head-on.

One of the most impactful tracks from the album was "Polygraph Eyes." This haunting song tackled the sensitive topic of sexual assault with unflinching honesty, shedding light on the prevalence of such incidents and the importance of consent. Its powerful message reverberated far and wide, sparking important conversations and giving a voice to survivors.

Another standout single from the album was "Loner." With its anthemic chorus and rebellious spirit, "Loner" became an anthem for those who felt marginalized or misunderstood by society. Yungblud's ability to capture the essence of youthful rebellion and defiance struck a chord with listeners, cementing his status as a voice for the disenfranchised.

As "21st Century Liability" continued to gain traction, Yungblud embarked on a relentless touring schedule, bringing his electrifying live performances to audiences around the world. His dynamic stage presence and unbridled energy captivated fans, earning him a reputation as one of the most exciting live acts in the industry.

But beyond the music, "21st Century Liability" represented something greater—a rallying cry for a generation grappling with the complexities of the modern world. Through his music, Yungblud offered a voice to the voiceless, a beacon of hope for those who felt marginalized or unheard.

In the next chapter, we will explore Yungblud's evolution beyond "21st Century Liability," from his collaborations with other artists to his growing impact on popular culture and activism. Join us as we delve deeper into the world of Yungblud, where music becomes a catalyst for change and rebellion is a way of life.

Chapter 5: The Underrated Youth and Collaborations

Following the success of his debut studio album, Yungblud continued to push the boundaries of his artistry with the release of his EP, "The Underrated Youth." Released in October 2019, this project served as a testament to Yungblud's commitment to amplifying the voices of the marginalized and underserved.

"The Underrated Youth" showcased Yungblud's evolution as both a musician and an activist, with tracks that explored themes of identity, mental health, and societal pressures. From the anthemic "Parents," which addressed the pressures of conformity and the importance of individualism, to the poignant "Hope For the Underrated Youth," a rallying cry for a generation struggling to be heard, each song on the EP resonated with authenticity and urgency.

In addition to his solo work, Yungblud also collaborated with a diverse range of artists, further expanding his sonic palette and amplifying his message. One of the most notable collaborations came in the form of "11 Minutes," a collaboration with Halsey and Travis Barker. This electrifying track, released in February 2019, explored the complexities of relationships and the fleeting nature of time, earning widespread acclaim for its raw emotion and infectious energy.

Yungblud's collaboration with Dan Reynolds of Imagine Dragons on "Original Me" further showcased his ability to tackle sensitive subjects with honesty and vulnerability. Released in October 2019, the song delved into themes of self-acceptance and the struggles of maintaining authenticity in an image-driven society, striking a chord with listeners around the world.

But perhaps most importantly, Yungblud used his platform as an artist to shine a light on pressing social issues and advocate for change. Through his music, he addressed topics such as mental health, gender identity, and political activism, encouraging his fans to speak out and take action.

In the next chapter, we will delve deeper into Yungblud's exploration of activism and social issues through his music, as well as his continued collaborations with other artists. Join us as we uncover the impact of Yungblud's work on popular culture and his ongoing efforts to effect positive change in the world.

Chapter 6: Weird! and Continued Success

In December 2020, Yungblud unleashed his second studio album, "Weird!," upon the world, signaling a new chapter in his musical journey. The album, aptly titled to reflect the surreal and unpredictable nature of the times, showcased Yungblud's evolution as an artist while maintaining the raw energy and rebellious spirit that had become his trademark.

"Weird!" was a sonic exploration of the chaos and uncertainty of the modern world, with Yungblud fearlessly tackling themes such as mental health, societal pressures, and the search for identity. The album's title track, "Weird!," served as a rallying cry for a generation grappling with the challenges of the COVID-19 pandemic and the upheaval it brought to daily life.

But "Weird!" was more than just an album; it was a testament to Yungblud's resilience and adaptability in the face of adversity. Despite the challenges posed by the pandemic, Yungblud refused to be silenced, using his music as a platform to connect with fans and spread messages of hope and solidarity.

Singles like "Weird!" and "Strawberry Lipstick" captivated audiences with their infectious hooks and unapologetic energy, earning Yungblud critical acclaim and commercial success. The album's dynamic blend of genres and styles showcased Yungblud's versatility as an artist, cementing his status as one of the most exciting voices in contemporary music.

In addition to his musical endeavors, Yungblud also embraced the challenges of the COVID-19 pandemic as an opportunity to innovate and connect with fans in new ways. From virtual concerts and live streams to interactive social media campaigns, Yungblud leveraged technology to stay connected with his audience and spread messages of positivity and resilience.

As the world navigated the uncertainty of the pandemic, Yungblud remained a beacon of hope and inspiration for his fans, reminding them that even in the darkest of times, music has the power to uplift and unite us.

In the next chapter, we will explore Yungblud's continued success and his ongoing efforts to effect positive change through his music and activism. Join us as we delve deeper into the world of Yungblud, where rebellion is a way of life and the pursuit of authenticity knows no bounds.

As Yungblud's career continued to soar, he remained steadfast in his commitment to using his platform for activism and social change. Through his music, performances, and public advocacy, Yungblud became a powerful voice for marginalized communities and a beacon of hope for young people around the world.

One of Yungblud's most notable endeavors was his participation in various social justice movements, including the Black Lives Matter protests following the murder of George Floyd in 2020. Yungblud not only attended these protests but also used his platform to amplify the voices of activists and advocate for racial equality and police reform.

In addition to his activism around racial justice, Yungblud also continued to address other pressing social issues through his music and advocacy. From LGBTQ+ rights to mental health awareness, Yungblud fearlessly tackled taboo subjects and sparked important conversations that resonated with his fans.

Furthermore, Yungblud's dedication to activism extended beyond his music and public appearances. He actively collaborated with organizations and charities that aligned with his values, donating his time and resources to causes that mattered to him. Whether it was supporting mental health initiatives or advocating for LGBTQ+ rights, Yungblud remained committed to making a positive impact on the world.

Despite his hectic schedule and the demands of his burgeoning career, Yungblud never lost sight of his responsibility as an artist and activist. He continued to push boundaries, challenge stereotypes, and inspire a new generation of changemakers to speak out and make a difference.

In the years to come, Yungblud's impact on popular culture and activism only continued to grow. His fearless spirit and unwavering commitment to authenticity endeared him to fans around the world, solidifying his status as a cultural icon and a force for positive change.

As we reflect on Yungblud's journey, it becomes clear that his legacy extends far beyond his music. He is not just an artist; he is a symbol of rebellion, resilience, and hope—a reminder that with passion, perseverance, and a little bit of chaos, anything is possible.

Chapter 7: Yungblud Era and Latest Projects

In 2022, Yungblud entered a new phase of his career with the release of his self-titled third studio album, "Yungblud." This album marked a significant evolution in his sound and artistic vision, showcasing a more mature and introspective side of the artist while retaining the raw energy and rebellious spirit that had defined his earlier work.

The album's lead single, "The Funeral," was a haunting reflection on mortality and the fleeting nature of life. Its dark, brooding sound and introspective lyrics struck a chord with listeners, earning praise for its emotional depth and raw honesty. The accompanying music video, starring Sharon Osbourne and Ozzy Osbourne, added to the song's impact, further solidifying Yungblud's reputation as a visionary artist unafraid to tackle complex themes.

Another standout track from the album was "Memories," a collaboration with American singer Willow. The song, with its infectious melody and heartfelt lyrics, became an instant hit, showcasing Yungblud's versatility as a songwriter and performer. The music video, featuring an appearance from YouTuber and Twitch streamer Valkyrae, further elevated the song's popularity, cementing its place as one of Yungblud's most beloved tracks.

In addition to his music, Yungblud also expanded his creative horizons into the world of film with the release of "Mars," a short film based on his 2020 song of the same name. The film, a collaboration between Mercury Studios and Interscope Films, focused on the story of a fan named Charlie Acaster who was struggling to convince her parents that she is transgender. Through "Mars," Yungblud used his platform to shed light on important social issues and advocate for LGBTQ+ rights, further solidifying his reputation as a socially conscious artist.

As Yungblud's career continued to flourish, so too did his activism efforts. From supporting mental health initiatives to advocating for LGBTQ+ rights and racial justice, Yungblud remained committed to using his platform for positive change. Through his music, his advocacy, and his unwavering dedication to authenticity, Yungblud continued to inspire a new generation of fans to speak out, stand up, and make a difference.

As we look to the future, it is clear that Yungblud's impact on popular culture and activism will only continue to grow. His fearless spirit, boundless creativity, and unwavering commitment to social justice make him not just a musician, but a cultural icon—a beacon of hope for a generation in need of change.

Chapter 8: Personal Life and Relationships

Beyond his public persona as Yungblud, Dominic Richard Harrison has been open about his personal struggles and experiences, offering fans a glimpse into his life beyond the stage.

One aspect of Yungblud's personal life that he has been candid about is his health struggles, particularly his battles with insomnia. In August 2018, Yungblud shared on social media that he struggles with insomnia, a condition that can have significant impacts on one's physical and mental well-being. Despite the challenges posed by this condition, Yungblud has remained resilient, using his music and advocacy work as outlets for expression and coping.

In addition to his health struggles, Yungblud has also been vocal about his exploration of his sexuality and relationships. In interviews, he has described himself as sexually fluid, indicating that he does not adhere to traditional labels or categories when it comes to his sexual orientation. This openness and willingness to defy societal norms have resonated with fans, many of whom appreciate Yungblud's authenticity and honesty.

One of Yungblud's most high-profile relationships was with American singer Halsey. The pair began dating in late 2018 and quickly became one of music's most talked-about couples. Their relationship garnered significant media attention, with fans eagerly following their every move. However, in October 2019, Halsey confirmed their breakup, stating that they had decided to remain friends. Despite the end of their romantic relationship, Yungblud and Halsey have continued to support each other professionally and remain on good terms.

Following his breakup with Halsey, Yungblud began dating American singer and fashion designer Jesse Jo Stark. The pair made their relationship public in June 2021, sharing glimpses of their life together on social media. Their relationship has been characterized by mutual support and admiration, with both artists celebrating each other's successes and accomplishments.

As Yungblud continues to navigate the ups and downs of fame and relationships, he remains committed to staying true to himself and sharing his experiences with his fans. Through his music and his openness about his personal life, Yungblud has inspired countless fans to embrace their own identities and live authentically, proving that vulnerability can be a source of strength and connection.

Chapter 9: Influences and Legacy

Yungblud's musical journey has been shaped by a diverse array of influences, spanning genres and generations. From rock and punk icons to pop and hip-hop pioneers, Yungblud's eclectic taste in music has informed his unique sound and artistic vision.

Among his influences are legendary artists such as Arctic Monkeys, Nirvana, and The Beatles, whose rebellious spirit and boundary-pushing approach to music have left an indelible mark on Yungblud's own work. He has also cited contemporary artists like Lady Gaga, Post Malone, and Kanye West as sources of inspiration, highlighting his appreciation for innovation and experimentation in music.

But perhaps most importantly, Yungblud's influences extend beyond the realm of music to include cultural and social icons who have challenged the status quo and inspired change. From Freddie Mercury and Mick Jagger to activists like Greta Thunberg and Malala Yousafzai, Yungblud draws inspiration from those who have used their platform to make a positive impact on the world.

Yungblud's impact on the music industry has been profound, challenging conventions and defying expectations at every turn. Through his fearless approach to songwriting, his electrifying performances, and his unwavering commitment to authenticity, Yungblud has carved out a unique space for himself in the industry, earning acclaim from critics and adoration from fans around the world.

As a boundary-pushing artist, Yungblud's legacy is one of rebellion, resilience, and authenticity. He has not only redefined what it means to be a rock star in the 21st century but has also inspired a new generation of musicians to embrace their individuality and speak out against injustice.

Looking to the future, Yungblud's aspirations are as bold and ambitious as ever. He continues to push the boundaries of his artistry, exploring new sounds, and collaborating with artists from diverse backgrounds. But above all, Yungblud remains committed to using his platform for good, advocating for social change, and inspiring others to do the same.

As we reflect on Yungblud's journey and legacy, one thing is clear: his impact on music and culture will be felt for generations to come. Through his music, his activism, and his unwavering commitment to authenticity, Yungblud has become more than just an artist—he is a symbol of hope, rebellion, and resilience in an ever-changing world.

Chapter 10: Conclusion

Yungblud's journey from a troubled youth in Doncaster to a global music sensation is nothing short of remarkable. Throughout his career, he has fearlessly challenged conventions, defied expectations, and used his platform to amplify the voices of the marginalized and underserved.

From his early days as an actor to his meteoric rise as a musician, Yungblud has never been afraid to speak his truth and confront societal issues head-on. Through his music, he has tackled topics ranging from mental health and sexuality to political activism and social justice, sparking important conversations and inspiring change.

Yungblud's impact on the music industry and popular culture cannot be overstated. His boundary-pushing sound, electrifying performances, and unwavering commitment to authenticity have earned him a devoted following and cemented his status as a cultural icon.

As he looks to the future, Yungblud's aspirations are as bold as ever. He continues to push the boundaries of his artistry, exploring new sounds and collaborating with artists from diverse backgrounds. But his commitment to activism and social change remains at the forefront of his mission, driving him to use his platform for good and inspire others to do the same.

In closing, Yungblud's journey is a testament to the power of music to uplift, unite, and effect change. As he continues to make his mark on the world, one thing is certain: his legacy will endure, inspiring generations to come to speak out, stand up, and make a difference.

Printed in Great Britain
by Amazon

46155839R00030